Ready or Not

poems by

Robin Wright

Finishing Line Press
Georgetown, Kentucky

Ready or Not

Copyright © 2019 by Robin Wright
ISBN 978-1-64662-303-7 First Edition
All rights reserved under International and Pan-American Copyright Conventions. No part of this book may be reproduced in any manner whatsoever without written permission from the publisher, except in the case of brief quotations embodied in critical articles and reviews.

ACKNOWLEDGMENTS

My deepest gratitude to the editors of the following journals and anthology where these poems were first published:

Amarillo Bay: "Renters"
Ariel Chart: "Breaking Up," and "Fringe"
Foliate Oak Literary Magazine: "A Night at Charlie's Place"
Indiana Voice Journal: "Side Trip"
Lost River Literary Magazine: "Services at a Later Date"
Muddy River Poetry Review: "After the Funeral"
Nature Writing: "Ghost Orchid"
Peacock Journal: "Trains in the Night"
Rat's Ass Review: "What This Woman Wants," and "After You Left"
See Spot Run: "Runaway"
Terror House Magazine: "In Memory of Randy H," and "Like This"
Zygote in My Coffee: "Sex and Margaritas"
"Alzheimer's" was published in *Time Present, Time Past*, the University of Southern Indiana's 50th anniversary anthology

I would also like to thank Jim McGarrah, Dianne Berry, Donna Hendricks, Karen DeWitt, Patti Easley, and the poets of the RAR online poetry critique group. Many of these poems needed a village, and I'm fortunate to have had the help of these fine writers.

Publisher: Leah Maines
Editor: Christen Kincaid
Cover Art: Robin Wright
Author Photo: Alisha Wright
Cover Design: Elizabeth Maines McCleavy

Order online: www.finishinglinepress.com
also available on amazon.com

Author inquiries and mail orders:
Finishing Line Press
P. O. Box 1626
Georgetown, Kentucky 40324
U. S. A.

Table of Contents

Fringe 1

What This Woman Wants 2

Renters 3

Sex and Margaritas 4

Side Trip 5

A Night at Charlie's Place 6

Breaking Up 7

After You Left 8

Like This 9

After the Funeral 10

Services at a Later Date 11

In Memory of Randy H 12

Ghost Orchid 13

Runaway 14

Trains in the Night 15

Alzheimer's 16

*This collection of poems is dedicated to
the memory of Patty Aakhus,
who encouraged me to take a poetry class.
Had it not been for her encouragement,
my poetry may have stayed locked inside of me.*

Fringe

In the seventies, I envied girls who wore
halter tops and hot pants. Hippy chicks

who wound their hair into a spiral
of desire, waiting to unfurl at a touch,

 wearing the space of long-haired guys,
dressed in tie-dyed t-shirts and Levi jeans.

I stood wrapped in a leather jacket,
raked my fingers across the fringe.

What This Woman Wants

I want to lie next to you, breathe
your animal smell, lick the side of your head
where skin and hair meet. I want to sip *White Zin*
until poetry pours through us
and you drink me in.
I want you to want me
like wind, blowing through you
not stopping, not slowing, shaking you
until you forget there's anything
outside the window, the room, the bed.

Renters

We're young, newly married,
and when the landlord hands us the key
to our first apartment, we're transported

into the car of a Disneyland ride,
the thrill rising to meet us
as we descend down the rail.

The baby in my womb is just a flutter now,
but we envision him swinging and flipping
on the jungle gym nearby.

Our thoughts carousel as we open the door
then freeze like wooden horses.
The apartment doesn't look like

the model. Bare floors, vacant windows,
curtain rods left hanging
by loose screws. A paper cup and bag

abandoned in the corner.
We promise each other we'll cover
floors, toss sheets over windows,

throw away the residue of another life,
and care for this baby
when he falls head first into birth.

Sex and Margaritas

The air an aroma of sizzling steak
and peppers, the sun a bikini of light.
Hunger springs
like a tiger from the gut of the jungle. You plunge
ice into tumblers, splash
Cuervo into the mix. The cubes dance
like stars somersaulting from their night sky portrait.
We stretch out on the porch like fat
gold cats, waiting
for more.

Side Trip

Our Chevy glides into a gas station
of some small town. We face
dirty windows, smudged doors,
rusty water pooling in the bathroom.

This stop not part of our vacation plans
but one we make, nearly empty,
paper maps out of date, our argument
long past its expiration.

An attendant tips the brim of his cap,
fills our tank, tells us about the 350
in his '69 Firebird, shakes his head,
says his wife moved in with the sheriff.

He longs to get away from this station.
If the lottery would just come through,
he'd take his *Bird* and fly right out of here.

He wipes grease from his hand. We shake it,
leave, think about Daytona Beach.
We'll swim, laugh, sip drinks with umbrellas,
offer a toast, *To Us*. But on our minds,
the gas station, the man, his escape.

A Night at Charlie's Place

Upstairs, a balcony snuggled above blue, red, and gold lights
that scintillate across the stage and dance floor,
above a globe light made of jig-saw-puzzle glass.

Later, people will be dancing in synchronized motion under those lights,
like glitter come to life, bodies leaning into one another,
heads nodding thanks to the band for a few less moments of loneliness.

I find a table in back of the twilight room,
order a shot of tequila, and hope this really is his last performance
with the young singer he thought he was in love with.

It's early.

The only patrons are tired men, lounging on stools
with well-settled grooves, sucking mugs of Bud from Charlie's tap.
Marlboro reds are within easy reach, and I wonder
how many years, marriages, and beers they consumed
before their choices made them weary.

Band members filter in for a sound check,
and the lead singer pours out lyrics of *Love Shack* through
bumble-bee buzzes and pig-squeal feedback. Nothing to do but

stop, adjust, try again. The man I still love
grabs a Gibson that looks like it's been dipped in an oil slick and breaks
out a lead on *Power of Love*. His fingers press and slide the strings;
his back arches under the weight of notes. The sounds ring through,
rise to share space with wafting smoke. I down the shot and wait.

Breaking Up

The Madrid Fault opened
her earthen mouth
and cried out.
Knees of buildings
shook like Jell-O.
Hearts of windows
tapped a quick pulse,
but you escaped
untouched.

After You Left

I dreamt I woke up blind
outside on hard ground,
unable to distinguish
one blade of grass from another.
All around me birds cooed,
as if they knew
your leaving didn't change
water, earth, or sky.
Sky still offered a breakfast
of sun and milky clouds.
Water still bathed the earth
to new hues of green and gray.
Earth still held me upright
though I wanted, in my blindness,
to fall upon her. And the birds,
the birds continued chanting
praise for the day.

Like This

Phone buzzes, buzzes, buzzes on my desk,
middle of the workday, displays my son's name.

I drop my pen and stare. This is not a text
like *KK, Sure,* or *Yes.*

My son calls, my brain flashes,
emergency, emergency, emergency.

My boss lets me take the call,
knows my son never calls like this.

He's upset about a Wisconsin company
ready to implant microchips

in hands, to unlock doors,
make a purchase, track location.

Wants my thoughts after he asks,
Who would agree to this?

A rice-sized pellet injected
into a hand, a hand like this,

like the one I'm using
to hold my phone.

After the Funeral

Shelves of books surround me
as I stare out a window.

*Rocky Mountains evicted
my uncle from his home
fashioned of cancer.*

Outside, trees boast elderly ecru
and infant green leaves.

*My brother and I battled
road construction, rain, and darkness
for sixteen hours straight.*

A jackhammer rumbles the corner
where a medical school graces the future.

*Uncle Mike, past but no longer present,
locked in the minds of those who viewed
his silent ash.*

Students will run to class, learn strategies to fight
bodies that strike back against themselves.

Services at a Later Date

I pick blue hydrangeas
from my yard. Don't know
what to do with them.
Arrange them in a vase, press
them in a book, release them
at the riverbank? My friend,
Gloria, gone six months.
Online obituary still says,
Services at a later date.

I pull off some petals, toss them
in the grass, wave stems
like impotent wands.
More petals fall. The ground
is loose and damp. I claw
the soil, bury what's left
of the flowers, push
my palms together, pretend
I know how to pray.

In Memory of Randy H

Hippo—your teenage nickname
said, shouted, mumbled, mouthed,
breath wandering into the world
in the days your orange Cutlass
performed pirouettes
in an iced parking lot,
laughter and Meatloaf's vocals
the backdrop for innocence
reflected in the glow
of dashboard light.

You flipped burgers, ladled chili, fried chicken
at Farmer's Daughter Restaurant
while customers grilled me about
latest specials, iced coffee, pumpkin pie.

Always a next joke or another prank
ready to be poured or played,
like the supposed secret in the walk-in freezer
whose door you closed on me.

My hands gripped my hips, hornet eyes
confronting when you opened the door,
sporting your smile, offering a hug.

Forty years later the local paper
spun your obituary, weaving the fabric
of your life. Cancer claimed you
at 55, a thread I've yet to grasp.

Ghost Orchid

Those few weeks of summer
after the sphinx moth strokes you with its tongue,
your slender white petals float from thin stems,
drifting in air, no leaves for a partner,
while your dark roots, barely visible, cling
to cypress, pop ash, or pond apple trees,
never touching ground, never appearing
connected to the earth.

Runaway

The girl, blonde hair touching her
bare shoulders like a whisper,

looks in the mirror. How long
since she watched her mother paint

lipstick over swollen lips
plaster powder on bruised skin?

She glances past her image
at the naked, balding man,

lying on sheets crumpled,
stained. She lights a Lucky

Strike as he jerks on pants, leaves
her slumped on the edge

of the bed, damp with sweat,
dirty with memories,

dissolving under the sign,
 Value Motel.

Trains in the Night

A low moan whispers through night's shaded room.
Faded walls, yellowed pages pay homage

to age. For years Sara's nighttime howl,
harmony for the train's refrain. Papery skin,

tulle of hair, now gone. Tracks spin her
memorial for miles, roses tossed along rails.

The train's requiem slow, sorrowful;
a low moan cries through the bruised night.

Alzheimer's

You stand on the sidewalk, head down,
staring at your shirt, twisted
blue lines running through black.
Your worn grey pants bag as you turn,
shuffle to the corner.

A block away, a fire truck's siren jolts
the air. Your gaze travels from black and blue
to screaming red, your bruised mind
trying to light a fire
of remembrance.

A yellow-bricked school beckons
from another direction, basketball goal
holding court in the schoolyard.
You reach out your hand,
pull it back
empty.

You pack that hand into your pocket,
stumbling away
from what you once knew.

Robin Wright lives in Southern Indiana and received a bachelor's degree in English from the University of Southern Indiana. Her work has appeared online and in print in various journals and anthologies, including *Panoply, Black Bough Poetry, Spank the Carp, Rue Scribe, Terror House Magazine, Rune Bear, Another Way Round, Ariel Chart, Bindweed Magazine, Muddy River Poetry Review* among others. She had a poem nominated for a Pushcart Prize by *Panoply*.

When she's not writing or working, she's spending time with her family, including her three grandchildren. She was once bestowed the title of Majestic Grandma by her granddaughter who enjoys, along with her younger brothers, being spoiled by Grandma.

www.ingramcontent.com/pod-product-compliance
Lightning Source LLC
LaVergne TN
LVHW041526070426
835507LV00013B/1846